Parasites & Partners

LODGERS AND CLEANERS

Bridget Giles

Raintree

Chicago, Illinois

Chicago, Illinois

First published 2003 by Raintree, a division of Reed Elsevier Inc.
© 2003 The Brown Reference Group plc

Library of Congress Cataloging-in-Publication Data

Giles, Bridget.
  Lodgers and cleaners / Bridget Giles.
    p. cm. — (Parasites and partners)
Summary: A comprehensive look at different types of creatures that live
with, or clean, other creatures and the benefits that these
relationships provide.
Includes bibliographical references and index.
  ISBN 0-7398-6991-4 (lib. bdg. : hardcover) — ISBN 1-4109-0358-3 (pbk.)
  1. Symbiosis—Juvenile literature. [1. Symbiosis. 2. Animals—Habits
and behaviors.] I. Title. II. Series.
  QH548.G56 2003
  577.8'5—dc21
                              2003007052

ISBN 1-4109-0358-3

Printed and bound in Singapore.
1 2 3 4 5 6 7 8 9 0 07 06 05 04 03 02

Acknowledgements

The publisher would like to thank the following for permission to use photographs:

Key: l – left, r – right, c – center, t – top, b – bottom.
Ardea: Thomas Dressler 23, Pascal Goetgheluck 17t, D. Parer & E. Parer-Cook 29, P Morris 16t; **Corbis:** Tim Davis 24b, Robert Yin 10b; **Charles Dill:** 30; **Jeff Jefford:** 11t, 11b, 4cb, 5t, 8t, 8b; **Dennis & Marlis Merbach:** 19tc, 19tr; **NHPA:** N. A. Callow 18–19, B. Jones & M. Shimlock 9, 12t, Stephen Kraseman 17b, Norbert Wu 26t; **New Zealand Tourist Board:** 28b; **Oxford Scientific Films:** 7, 13b, 15, 26b, Michael Fogden 20t, D. J. Saunders 28t; **PHIL:** CDC/Janice Carr 4b; **Photodisc:** Frank & Joyce Burek 5b, Photolink 16b; **Still Pictures:** Fred Bavendam 25, Jacques Jangoux 5 (background), Luiz C. Marigo 20b; **USDA/ARS:** 4ct, Jack Dykinga 4t; **Front Cover: NHPA:** B. Jones & M. Shimlock (t); **Ardea:** Thomas Dressler (b).

For The Brown Reference Group plc

Project Editor: Jim Martin
Consultancy Board: Dr. Robert S. Anderson,
    Royal Canadian Museum of Nature, Ottawa, Canada;
    Prof. Marilyn Scott, Institute of Parasitology,
    McGill University, Montreal, Canada
Designed by: Pewter Design Associates
Illustrator: Mike Woods
Picture Researcher: Helen Simm
Managing Editor: Bridget Giles
Art Director: Dave Goodman
Production Director: Alastair Gourlay

For Raintree

Editor: Jim Schneider
Managing Editor: Jamie West
Production Manager: Brian Suderski

Front cover: In defense, a boxer crab waves its claws, on
which stinging sea anemones live (*top*); oxpeckers feed
on parasites on the body of a water buffalo (*bottom*).

Title page: This tarantula shares its burrow with a
type of frog. The frog keeps parasitic wasps away
from the spider's eggs.

Note to the Reader
Some words are shown in bold, like **this.** You can find out what they mean by looking in "Words to Know."

Parasites & Partners
LODGERS AND CLEANERS

Contents

Introduction

Animals and plants do not live alone. They are always interacting with other creatures. A close association between different species is called a **symbiosis.** *Parasites & Partners* introduces you to symbiotic relationships. You can see examples of these around you every day. Anyone who keeps a dog shares a symbiosis with their pet. The dog is fed and housed by its owner, who gains a companion and protection in return. Both partners in this relationship benefit, but that is not always the case. The different types of symbioses covered in this book are discussed in the box below.

Each book in *Parasites & Partners* looks at a different group of relationships. Find out how plants and animals interact with other types of creatures as they feed, breed, keep clean, find a home, and move around.

4

Some important words for you to remember

Symbiosis
A relationship between two different types of creatures is called a symbiosis. This bee is taking nectar from the flower to provision its nest, while the plant is using the bee to spread its pollen. Both partners benefit in this symbiosis.

Mutualism
Biologists call a relationship where both partners benefit a **mutualism.** Leaf-cutter ants provide food in the form of chewed-up leaves and a safe home for their fungus partners. The ants get to eat parts of the fungi in return.

Commensalism
A relationship in which one **organism** benefits but the other neither profits nor suffers is called a **commensalism.** One of the partners is usually called a **host.** Here, a crinoid shrimp blends in with the colors of its feather star host.

Parasite
A creature that benefits at the expense of another but does not usually kill it is called a **parasite.** The organism it attacks is called a **host.** This flea is a rat parasite. It lives on the body of a rat and feeds on its blood.

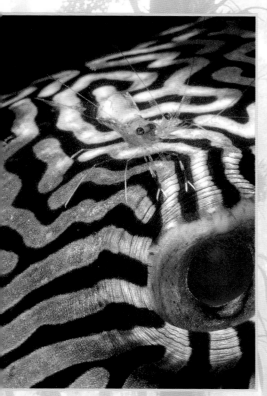

▶ *This cloud forest tree is dotted with bromeliads. Discover plants that provide homes for other creatures on pages 14–21.*

◀ *A shrimp searches for food on a pufferfish. Explore the world of animals that clean on pages 22–29.*

In **this** book...

...you will look at creatures that live with or clean other animals and plants, and the benefits that these partnerships provide. In chapter one, find out about animals that share their homes and even their bodies with other types of animals. **Coral** reefs are rich in these sorts of relationships. Discover plants that provide homes for other creatures in chapter two. Some of these lodgers, such as ants, protect the plant, which provides sugary nectar in return.

In the final chapter, we discover how animals provide cleaning services by nibbling at dirt and parasites. Some cleaners live on the bodies of their clients, but others, such as cleaner wrasse, set up cleaning "shops," where larger fish gather.

▲ *A clown fish nestles in the fronds of its sea anemone host. Learn about animal lodgers on pages 6–13.*

Animal **LODGERS**

Animals form strange relationships that cross the boundaries of type, size, and behavior. These relationships often involve shelter and protection for one or both of the partners. Symbioses like these often take place beneath the surface of the sea.

6

In warm, shallow seas around the world, tiny animals called **coral** polyps build coral reefs. These reefs are made from layers of dead coral skeletons. Only the top layer is living coral. Coral reefs are like underwater cities, busy with animal traffic day and night. Thousands of colorful creatures live on a reef, from fish and shrimps to sponges, starfish, and sea urchins. Danger is all around, but the reef offers safety and shelter.

Protectors

Perhaps the best-known coral reef partners are clown fish and their sea anemone **hosts.** The stripy clown fish is just one of many types of anemone fish. Sea anemones have lots of **tentacles** armed with stinging cells. They use the cells to stun prey. The anemone fish have a coating of thick, sticky mucus that masks their presence. This makes the fish invisible to the sea anemone. **Predators** of the fish are kept away by the stinging tentacles. The sea anemone eats leftovers from the fish's meals, and the fish also helps keep its host clean. Since both partners benefit, this relationship is called a **mutualism.**

▼ These fish are not hurt by the powerful stings of a Portuguese man o'war. They hide among its tentacles, safe from enemies.

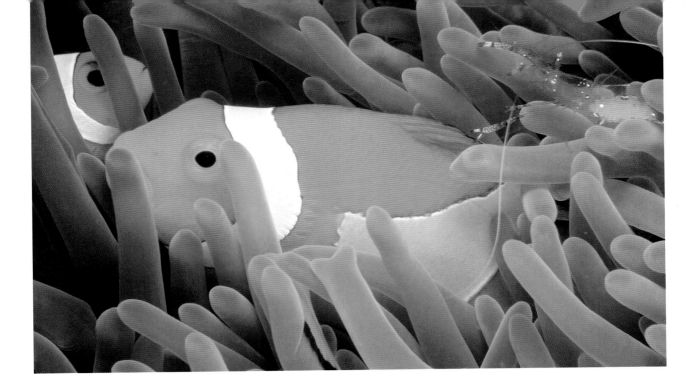

▲ *This pair of clown fish share their protective sea anemone home with an anemone shrimp.*

Fish are not the only animals protected by sea anemones. The tentacles provide a hideout for many shrimps, as well as tiny porcelain crabs. These crabs filter food from the water and are unharmed by the stinging cells of their hosts.

Some small fish shelter among the tentacles of creatures such as jellyfish and even the deadly Portuguese man o' war. Man o' war fish are immune to their host's stingers. They hide within the fringe of tentacles, which they nibble for food.

▶ *Porcelain crabs live within folds of sea anemone flesh. They filter food from the water with combs of threadlike filaments on their legs.*

Friendly shrimps

Shrimp gobies are small fish that live with snapping shrimps in burrows dug by the shrimps. Such pairs usually live in places with sandy seabeds. The shrimp is a good digger, so it builds the home and also keeps it clean. But the shrimp cannot see very well, and this is where the goby helps out. The goby stands guard when the pair ventures out from the burrow—the fish to feed, and the shrimp to repair the entrance. Outside, the shrimp keeps a sensitive **antenna** on one of the goby's flanks. If the fish spots a **predator,** it flicks its tail several times to warn its shrimp partner. Both dive into the burrow until it is safe to come out again.

9

▲ A flag-tail goby keeps watch while its snapping shrimp housemate makes repairs.

Goby guests

A wide range of undersea animals are hosts for gobies, including corals, sponges, and

Pea crabs

Pea crabs live in the Pacific and Atlantic oceans. When they are young, most pea crabs wriggle into the shell of a living bivalve, such as an oyster, clam, or mussel. Some pea crabs live inside other animals, such as sea cucumbers. Once inside the host, pea crabs are protected from fish and other animals that like to eat crabs. At first, the crabs come and go easily, but the females soon grow too big to leave. They only get to be about half an inch (1.3 cm) long but are still about three times bigger than the tiny males. Often soft and pea- or beanlike in shape, the crabs match the host's pale flesh in color. Male pea crabs have flat bodies, so they can still slip in and out of the shellfish even when fully grown.

The hosts of pea crabs feed on tiny scraps of food they sieve from the water. A pea crab living inside a shellfish feeds by helping itself to some of its host's food.

Fierce housemates

Some animals share their homes with fearsome creatures. In the deserts of the southern United States and in parts of Peru, some narrowmouth frogs live with tarantulas. Normally, the large spider eats small frogs, but its housemate is a special case. The pair lives together in a burrow, which the frog keeps free of ants, parasitic wasps, and many other insects that might attack the spider's eggs. The spider has a venomous bite and barbed hairs on its body. It rubs its back legs on its body to release a shower of hairs. These irritate the eyes, nose, and mouth of enemies like foxes. With these defenses, both spider and frog are safe from predators.

▲ *A tarantula and its frog house guest are perfect partners.*

even spiny sea urchins. Coral gobies come in all the colors of the rainbow. Each lives only on a certain type of coral. The gobies measure less than 1 inch (2.5 cm) long. Some have a sucker on their underside that keeps them securely attached to the coral below. The goby gets a safe place to live, but the host gains little. This is called a **commensal** relationship.

The color of a particular goby, whether it be bright red, yellow, or pink with blue spots, depends on the color of its host coral. Because the colors and patterns of goby and coral match so well, it can be very hard for a predator to spot a coral goby at home. The fish often spends its whole life on the coral, even laying its eggs there.

▼ *Coral gobies cling tightly to their hosts with suckers on their underside.*

Crab disguisers

Decorator crabs are masters of disguise. They grab small reef animals, such as sea squirts, sea anemones, and coral polyps, and attach them to their shells. As the house guests grow, they cover the crab's body. This provides perfect **camouflage** amid the clutter of a reef.

Some hermit crabs also keep gardens of creatures on their shells. These crabs live in the empty shells of animals such as whelks. Other hermit crabs look like they have fur growing on their shells. The "fur" is really a carpet of tiny animals called hydroids, which camouflage the crabs. Anemone hermit crabs attach sea anemones to their shells, often several at a time. The sea anemones get a place to live

Life with the stars

At night, some of the most colorful coral reef residents come out to feed. These are the feather stars. They look like large flowers, with up to 200 frondlike arms. But they are actually animals, and are relatives of starfish and sea urchins. Feather stars are home to many other creatures, from tiny clingfish and squat lobsters to shrimps and worms. These lodgers often match their host's colors and are hard for predators to spot. Ambon shrimps live only on feather stars. They can slowly change their colors to match those of their host exactly.

Feather stars are good places to live since they contain bad-tasting chemicals and have very little juicy flesh, so most fish leave them alone.

▲ *A crinoid shrimp closely matches the color of the feather star on which it lives. This species even has speckles, just like its host.*

▶ *These decorator crabs are preparing to mate. Their bodies are covered with sponges, sea squirts, and sea anemones.*

11

◀ *Anemones live on the claws of this boxer crab. The crab waves them at enemies. The sea anemones feed on scraps of the crab's food.*

▼ *These social shrimps live inside a sponge. The soldier guards the queen and other nest mates from invaders.*

12

and morsels of the crab's food. The crab is protected by the sea anemones' stinging tentacles.

When the hermit has grown so much it has to move to a larger shell, it takes its partners with it. The crab massages the base of each sea anemone until it lets go. Some sea anemones move themselves, slowly inching across to their new home.

A fistful of tentacles

Boxer crabs carry sea anemones in their claws. They wave their claws at attackers, which are scared off by the crab's fistfuls of stingers. This relationship is very important for the crabs. Their front pincers are shaped to help them carry their friends. Most crabs use these claws to catch food and rip it up. A boxer crab uses its second pair of legs to catch and mince food instead.

Sociable shrimps

Perhaps the most remarkable animal lodger is a type of shrimp from Central American waters. They spend their entire lives inside sponges, feeding on tissues from the walls of the water channels inside the sponge. Just like an ant or bee colony, each sponge contains a queen that produces all

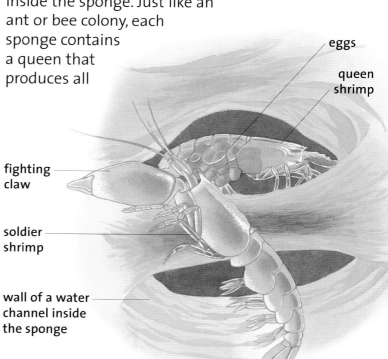

eggs

queen shrimp

fighting claw

soldier shrimp

wall of a water channel inside the sponge

of the young. The other shrimps do not breed but take care of their queen instead.

The shrimps must defend their sponge fiercely from other animals. Male soldiers guard the colony. They use their massive claw to fight other shrimps. They can also click the claw to produce a high-speed blast of water that drives enemies away.

Bottom-living fish

Sea cucumbers are strange animals. They have rings of frilly tentacles around their mouths, and some are incredibly colorful. Also, they breathe through their bottoms. The animal sucks in seawater through its anus, and oxygen is taken in before the water is forced out again. One fish, the pearlfish, lives inside sea cucumbers. As the cucumber breathes in, the fish slips inside and lodges itself inside the sea cucumber. The fish spends the day inside, coming out at night to feed on small crabs and shrimps.

The pearlfish gains a safe place to live. Most predators steer clear of sea cucumbers since they contain poisons. The fish will nibble on its host's organs. Luckily, the sea cucumber can soon grow them back.

KEY FACTS

■ Many animals live with other species (types) for shelter and protection. These relationships are mutualisms if both partners benefit.

■ Many animals that lodge with others live beneath the surface of the sea, often on coral reefs.

■ The animals that live on feather stars do not benefit or harm their hosts. This is a type of commensal relationship.

■ Some lodgers, such as the pearlfish that live inside the bodies of sea cucumbers, are unwelcome irritants.

▼ *A pearlfish wriggles inside the body of a sea cucumber as it draws in water to breathe.*

13

Plant **HOTELS**

Plants are important providers of food to many animals, but some provide room and board, too. Ant-plants form unique ties with their guests, and other plants are like miniature villages, providing homes to many different creatures.

14

Even if you've never been to east or southern Africa, you're sure to recognize the animals of their **savannas** (grasslands), such as elephants, lions, and zebras. Yet some of the savannas' most interesting residents are hundreds of times smaller than these huge beasts. These are the acacia ants.

Thorn sweet thorn

Savannas are grasslands with scattered trees and shrubs. Among the most common of the savanna trees are acacias. The branches of some are covered in hollow thorns. These stop browsing animals from munching on the trees. The thorns also serve another purpose—acacia ants live inside them. The ants get a safe home away from animals that might eat them. Like guests in a nice hotel, the ants also get room service. The acacia tree secretes sugary **nectar** from the bases of its leaves to feed the ants. The tree also supplies ant-sized buttons called **Beltian bodies.** These are a good source of protein.

If the ants spot a plant sending up shoots near their acacia tree, they will snip the shoots off

◀ *These acacia ants are harvesting Beltian bodies, nutritious buttons provided by the acacia tree for its ants.*

ant group's nest. Keeping plants from growing nearby helps prevent such raids. Whatever the origin of this behavior, the tree benefits since it does not have to compete with other plants for the limited nutrition and water available in the poor savanna soil.

Acacia ants are fearsome fighters. Even army ants give their trees a wide berth. If the acacia ants spot an animal trying to eat the leaves of their home, they will attack it mercilessly, no matter how big the browser is. Hordes of acacia ants bite and sting the browser again and again. They do not stop attacking until the enemy is driven away to look for something less

▲ Ants live inside this acacia thorn. The little hole is the entrance to the ants' nest.

with their sharp mouthparts. This behavior might have begun as a way to keep other ants from moving on to their tree. Trespassing ants could use such plant bridges to enter and attack the first

▲ Giraffes cannot browse for long on an acacia tree, since the tree's ant defenders deliver painful stings.

◄ When acacia trees flower, the flowers release chemicals that repel ants. This allows other insects to reach the pollen inside the flowers without being attacked by the acacia ants.

well defended. Insects that try to munch on the leaves are captured and killed.

Other ant hotels

Acacias are not the only plants that provide ant lodgings. Piper plants have hollow leaves inside which colonies of ants live. The ants keep browsing insects away. The plant secretes tiny blobs of nutrient-rich food in return.

Ant-house plants have swollen stems filled with tunnels that make great homes for ants.

▶ *The tiny white dots inside this piper plant are food provided by the plant for its ants.*

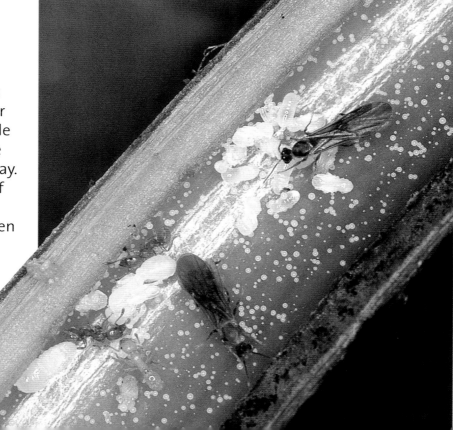

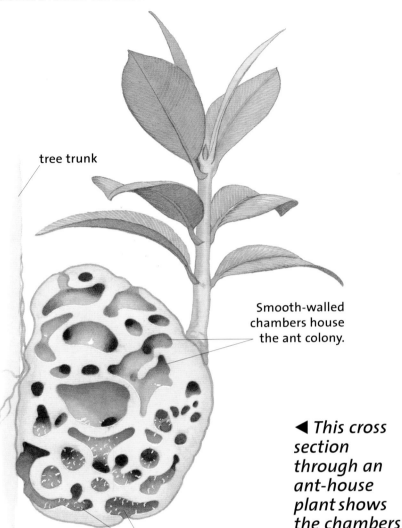

tree trunk

Smooth-walled chambers house the ant colony.

Ants dump their trash in warty-walled chambers.

◀ *This cross section through an ant-house plant shows the chambers where the ants live.*

Depending on the type of plant, the ants either hollow out the tunnels or the plant provides them ready made. Smooth-walled chambers are used for rearing the young ants. Other chambers with warty walls act as garbage dumps. The ants leave feces and discarded bits of their insect prey in these chambers. The plant absorbs nutrients from the ants' trash

through the warts. Living with ants allows ant-house plants to grow in places where there are few nutrients available.

Larger lodgers

Other animals sometimes lodge inside ant-house plants. Frogs and lizards, for example, often occupy the larger chambers. In northern Australia, caterpillars of the Apollo jewel butterfly live only inside the swollen stems of a particular ant-house plant. The caterpillars feed on the plant's leaves.

Unlike acacia ants, most ant-house plant ants are poor security guards that run from danger. The ants that live inside some rattan vines, however, are much fiercer. If an animal bumps

▶ *This orchid lives on the branch of a tree in the cloud forest of the Himalayas in Asia.*

18

Meat-eating ant-houses

Pitcher plants add nutrients to their diet by feasting on insects that fall into a liquid-filled bowl of leaves. One type of pitcher plant, *Nepenthes*, lures insects to their doom by secreting nectar from a pair of fanglike stalks hanging from a lid above the bowl. Insects tumble into the liquid below and are slowly broken down by chemicals. The plant then absorbs the nutrients. *Nepenthes* shares a remarkable relationship with one type of ant. The plants house the ants in their stems, providing food and nectar. In return,

▶ *The resident ants deal with a* **Nepenthes**-*eating weevil.*

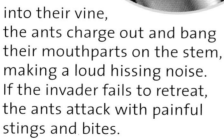

the ants fight off a weevil that likes to eat the pitcher plant. The ants sometimes climb down into the bowl to snatch a dead insect and can even swim through the liquid in search of food.

▼ *A Nepenthes plant's "fangs" bear nectar.*

into their vine, the ants charge out and bang their mouthparts on the stem, making a loud hissing noise. If the invader fails to retreat, the ants attack with painful stings and bites.

Plants on plants

All plants need water and sunlight to live. Most need soil, too. Soil provides vital nutrients and supports the plant so it can grow. However, there are some unusual plants that do not need soil. These are called **epiphytes.** Instead of growing in the ground, epiphytes grow on the branches and trunks of other plants. Most types of orchids are epiphytes. Many South American epiphytes belong to a group of plants called the bromeliads.

Orchids and bromeliads are common in rain forests, especially in cloud forests. Cloud forests grow high up on the sides of mountains in tropical regions. High temperatures and rainfall combine to produce permanent clouds of moisture.

Epiphytes cling to the trunks and branches of trees high in the **canopy.** The host tree does not benefit from the partnership in any way, but the epiphyte gains a place to live.

19

up to 5 gallons (20 liters) of water. That's about as much water as you use to take a bath!

Epiphyte aquariums

Bromeliads provide homes for many different types of creatures that live in the pools and between the leaves. Minute single-celled **organisms,** such as **bacteria** and algae, float in their waters. Other bromeliad dwellers include water fleas and seed shrimps that feed on tiny particles in the water. They, in turn, provide food for young insects such as mosquitoes,

Air plants and tanks

Epiphytes are either air plants or water collectors. Most orchids are air plants. They absorb all the water and nutrients they need from the air through their leaves and exposed roots.

Water collectors do things differently. Their sword-shaped leaves overlap at the base, creating bowls where rainwater collects. Rainwater runs off the tree above, picking up nutrients as it flows over leaves and branches. The plants absorb nutrients from the water that gathers in the bowls. Dead and dying insects and decaying leaves and twigs add to the nutritious broth.

Tank bromeliads have a large central cup that collects water. A large tank bromeliad can hold

▲ *A female strawberry poison dart frog carries one of its tadpoles on its back. The frog will take the tadpole to a pool formed by bromeliad leaves.*

▶ *Water that collects between the leaves of this bromeliad provides a home for many small rain forest creatures.*

Bromeliad nurseries

Jamaican bromeliad crabs use the pools of bromeliads as nurseries for their young. Unlike nearly all other crabs, a female bromeliad crab cares for her young. Before laying her eggs in a pool, the female crab kills any insect **larvae** living in the pool to stop them from eating the eggs. She removes garbage and mixes the water from time to time to ensure it is full of **oxygen**. The female will even carry snail shells into the pool. The snail

◄ A female crab brings a millipede to a bromeliad pool to feed her young.

shells release a chemical called **calcium carbonate** into the water of the bromeliad pool. The young crabs need this chemical to build their hard outer coverings. The female crab also provides food for her young. She catches small animals from the forest, such as millipedes. She rips prey into bite-sized chunks with her claws. The crab mother leaves the pieces in the pool to feed her offspring.

water bugs, and damselflies. Many frog tadpoles develop in bromeliad pools. Strawberry poison dart frogs lay a small clutch of eggs on a leaf. When an egg hatches, the tadpole wriggles onto the back of an adult.

The adult carries the tadpole to a bromeliad. Each tadpole is taken to a different pool; if they were all left in one pool the tadpoles would eat each other. The adult female lays eggs that do not hatch for the tadpoles to feed on, and the tadpoles also catch young insects.

KEY FACTS

■ Ant-plants live with ants. They include acacia trees, piper plants, and ant-house plants.

■ Tiny holes in the thorns of whistling thorn acacias allow the ants to get in. When the wind blows, the thorns whistle.

■ Up to 30,000 ants may live on a single acacia.

■ Ant-house plants provide homes for ants inside their swollen stems.

■ Epiphytes are plants that grow on other plants.

■ Young frogs, insects, and even some crabs develop in pools formed by bromeliad leaves.

Animal**CLEANERS**

If you've been camping or hiking you'll know that keeping clean in the great outdoors can be tricky. The same is true for animals, and they care more about hygiene than you might realize. Many use other animals to help them keep clean and free from parasites.

Animal cleaners occur virtually everywhere, from rain forest trees to **coral** reefs. Cleaning relationships are usually **mutualisms**; one partner has dirt and **parasites** removed, while the other gets a free meal and sometimes a place to live, too.

A lot of the animals that live on corals and sea anenomes help keep their **hosts** clean by eating parasites and bits of dirt. On land, ants' nests are home to many different animals that help clean the nest. In Central America, some rodents (the group that includes rats and mice) travel around with mobile teams of pest-control beetles. Rove beetles help keep a mouse burrow clear of fleas and other pests. When the mouse is on the move, the rove beetles hang on to its fur. One mouse might carry up to ten beetles arranged around its neck. Each of the beetles is up to a tenth of the length of the mouse, so this necklace of beetles can be very large!

Some other rodents have unusual insect cleaners. Blind, wingless *Hemimerus* earwigs are very different from

▲ *Yellow-billed oxpeckers gather on an African buffalo. The birds remove ticks and other pests from the buffalo's body.*

◀ A cleaner earwig scuttles around the neck of a giant pouched rat. The earwig feeds on fungi and dead skin within the rat's fur.

24

any other earwigs. They live only on the bodies of the world's largest rats, the giant pouched rats of west Africa. The earwigs hang on with strong claws. They keep the rats clean by feeding on **fungi** and bits of dead skin.

Accidental cleaners

Animals do not always realize that cleaners are around. In Texas, screech owls pluck snakes from the ground at night and bring them back to their nest. They sometimes catch blind snakes. These have smooth slippery skin and often wriggle free of the owl's claws as it tries to feed its young. Having avoided becoming lunch for the the owl

▶ A screech owl peers out through a tree hole—its nest is inside. The nest may be cleaned by a blind snake.

chicks, the blind snake burrows into the nest. There, it feeds on fly **larvae** (young) and other parasites, keeping the nest clean.

Fish cleaners

Fish cannot clean themselves. They can do little more than rub against rocks or other hard surfaces if they have an itch. In the busy underwater cities of coral reefs, however, some animals use this to their advantage. Certain fish and shrimps provide cleaning services for fish. The cleaners set up shop at a prominent place, like a large rock or a coral head on a reef. This becomes their cleaning station. The cleaners' clients gather there to be cleaned, patiently waiting their turn. Often the client fish include aggressive **predators** that would not normally hesitate to snack on such small fish or shrimps. At cleaning time, though, the predators do not attack. Some even change color to show that they want to be cleaned or to make their parasites stand out more clearly. Floating head up or head down is another sign that a fish wants to be cleaned.

The cleaner fish or shrimps nibble at parasites such as sea lice, as well as bits of dead skin and any damaged flesh.

▲ *This tomato grouper fish is allowing a cleaner shrimp to wander around its mouth in search of parasites.*

▲ Clients such as this lizard fish allow cleaner wrasse to nibble around their bulging, sensitive eyes.

The client fish hovers in the water, opening its mouth and **gills** wide to allow the cleaner access to these sensitive areas. Cleaner shrimps clamber all over their hosts to get at the tasty dirt and parasites.

A touching story

Touching is an important part of the cleaning process. A cleaner wrasse not only nibbles but also strokes the client fish with its body. The more the client fish are touched by the cleaners,

▶ A saber-tooth blenny pretends to be a cleaner. It fools another fish into coming close. The blenny then bites a chunk out of its victim.

Cleaners-to-go

Mites are tiny relatives of spiders that often live on other creatures as parasites, sucking their blood or eating flakes of skin. Some bees, however, live with mites that provide

cleaning mite

mite pouch

gut

queen bee

cleaning services. The mites feed on trash that would otherwise clutter up the nest. When a new queen bee leaves to start her own nest, the mites climb aboard. They hang on to her until they reach their new home. Some carpenter bees keep mites that lay eggs on the bee larvae. When the eggs hatch, the young mites keep the bee larvae free of fungi. The queens of these bees have pouches inside their bodies. The bee queens carry some mites in their pouches when they fly away to found a new nest.

◀ *A queen carpenter bee has a pouch for carrying tiny cleaning mites.*

the longer they hang around. Also, bigger and more aggressive fish are stroked for a longer time by the cleaner wrasse. Touching may signal that the job is not finished, or it may just soothe the clients and stop them from eating the cleaners. Some wrasse practice hit-and-run cleaning. They dart in, eat a few parasites, and shoot away. These fish do not stroke their clients, and perhaps that is why they clean so quickly.

Once bitten...

Cleaner fish have distinctive markings, such as stripes and bold colors, so their clients can recognize them easily. Some sneaky fish take advantage of this. The saber-tooth blenny, for example, looks just like a cleaner wrasse, with a long, dark stripe running from mouth to tail. Fish approach the blenny to be cleaned. But instead of removing troublesome parasites, the sabertooth darts forward and slices out a chunk of flesh before the larger fish realizes that it has been fooled.

Tricking cleaners

It is not always clients that are tricked—sometimes the roles are reversed. Many birds perform an activity called anting. During anting, a bird settles on an anthill and spreads its wings flat on the ground. Ants pour out from the anthill to repel the enemy. The ants clamber all over the bird,

shooting acids and other defensive chemicals from glands in their bodies. The chemicals do not harm the bird but they do kill mites, lice, and fungi that would otherwise dirty the bird's feathers. The bird may even pick up individual ants in its bill and use them to preen problem areas. The ants gain nothing from this relationship, but the bird benefits by having fewer parasites and an easy meal—it may eat some of the ants afterward.

◀ *This European jay is anting on a wood ants' nest.*

28

A parrot in sheep's clothing

Kea parrots live in the mountains of New Zealand. These dark green birds can eat practically anything and are known for their inventiveness and cunning. When winter comes, food can be scarce. So the parrots sometimes set up shop as sheep cleaners, plucking small parasites such as ticks from the woolly fleece.

▶ *The sharp bill of a kea can pierce a sheep's skin.*

At first, the sheep is grateful for this service, but once it has been fully cleaned of parasites, things can turn nasty. Finding that its host has run out of snacks, the kea may turn to the sheep itself for a meal. The parrot uses its beak to gouge a deep hole in the sheep's flesh. As it hangs on to the wool around the sheep's tail with its clawed feet, the parrot feeds on the fat around the sheep's kidneys.

Vampire oxpeckers?

In the grasslands of Africa, oxpecker birds clamber over large mammals such as buffaloes, rhinos, and giraffes to pick off pesky parasites such as ticks and lice. Oxpeckers have a flat bill for probing fur and long toes for hanging on. Their stiff tail acts as a supporting prop.

People have long thought of oxpeckers as helpful cleaners, but there is a downside to the relationship. The birds sometimes peck at open wounds and drink the blood. This can stop the wounds from healing properly and might cause infection.

Many other birds act as cleaners. Egyptian plovers are living toothbrushes that peck away pieces of trapped food from between the teeth of Nile crocodiles. Cattle egrets provide a similar service for large mammals farther south in Africa, while finches on the Galápagos Islands clean tiny parasites from wrinkles in the skin of giant tortoises and iguanas.

KEY FACTS

■ Most cleaning relationships are mutualisms. One partner has parasites and dirt removed, while the other gets a free meal.

■ Cleaner wrasse advertise their services with contrasting bands of blue and black on their bodies.

■ Many birds fool ants into cleaning them with their defensive chemicals.

■ Oxpeckers and egrets clean away parasites from large mammals.

■ Some mites help keep insect nests free of egg predators and parasites.

▼ *This Galápagos ground finch is resting on the head of a basking land iguana.*

29

Things to Do

Looking at lodgers

It is unlikely that you will see many of the **symbioses** this book covers in the wild. Unless, that is, you are lucky enough to be planning a trip to the grasslands of Africa, a South American rain forest, or a **coral** reef. If you visit your nearest aquarium, however, you might see anemone fish and some hermit crabs.

30

◀ You can buy airplants such as this one from florists.

You may be able to find examples of partners that provide lodgings around you. In the South, people grow bromeliads in their yards, and several types of bromeliads grow in the wild. Find a good field guide to identify different types of wild bromeliads.

You can often see bromeliads in florists, and people keep them as decorative houseplants. These types are unlikely to have many lodgers but are still fascinating.

In the wild, most **epiphytes** live on trunks and branches, but you don't need a giant rain forest tree in your bedroom to grow your own! Save up for an airplant. These are easy to look after. All they need to survive is a spray with a mister once in a while.

Books and websites

■ Green, Jen. *Small Worlds: Coral Reef.* New York: Crabtree, 2002.

■ Silverstein, Alvin, Virginia Silverstein, and Laura Silverstein Nunn, *Symbiosis (Science concepts)*. Brookfield, CT: Millbrook Press, 1998.

■ *Make your own paper bromeliad and find out more about tank bromeliads and their rain forest guests at* http://www.rainforest-alliance.org/kids%26teachers/kids/activities/index.html

Words to Know

antenna
One of a pair of sensitive feelers on the heads of animals such as insects and shrimps

bacteria
Very small single-celled organisms

Beltian body
Food button provided by an acacia tree for its ants

calcium carbonate
Chemical that many animals need to build strong shells

camouflage
Disguise that helps an animal blend into the background

canopy
Part of a forest formed by the leaves and branches near the treetops

commensalism
Relationship between two creatures in which one benefits but the other is unaffected

coral
Small animals that filter food from the water and form reefs in shallow seas

epiphyte
Plant that lives on another plant

fungus
Plantlike organism; mushrooms are a well-known example (plural: fungi)

gills
Feathery organs used by many underwater animals to draw oxygen from the water

host
Animal or plant that supports a parasite or a commensal organism

larva
Young of an insect such as a fly (plural: larvae)

mutualism
Relationship between two creatures in which both partners benefit

nectar
Sugary liquid produced by plants to reward pollinators

organism
Any type of living thing, including plants, animals, bacteria, and fungi

oxygen
Gas that all animals and plants need to live

parasite
Any organism that benefits at the expense of another

predator
Animal that hunts and eats other animals

savanna
Grassland with scattered trees in a hot region

symbiosis
Close relationship between different types of creatures (plural: symbioses)

tentacle
One of a series of long, flexible arms used by many animals to grab food

Index

Numbers in *italics* refer to pictures

32